NEW VANGUARD 239

NILE RIVER GUNBOATS 1882–1918

ANGUS KONSTAM   ILLUSTRATED BY PETER DENNIS

First published in Great Britain in 2016 by Osprey Publishing,
PO Box 883, Oxford, OX1 9PL, UK
1385 Broadway, 5th Floor, New York, NY 10018, USA
E-mail: info@ospreypublishing.com

Osprey Publishing, part of Bloomsbury Publishing Plc

A CIP catalogue record for this book is available from the British Library.

Print ISBN: 978 1 4728 1476 0
PDF ebook ISBN: 978 1 4728 1477 7
ePub ebook ISBN: 978 1 4728 1478 4

Index by Zoe Ross
Typeset in Sabon and Myriad Pro
Map by Nick Buxey
Originated by PDQ Media, Bungay, UK
Printed in China through World Print Ltd

16 17 18 19 20 10 9 8 7 6 5 4 3 2 1

Osprey Publishing supports the Woodland Trust, the UK's leading woodland
conservation charity. Between 2014 and 2018 our donations are being
spent on their Centenary Woods project in the UK.

www.ospreypublishing.com

Title page image: The Egyptian government gunboat *Bordein* in action near
Khartoum in 1885, after the city was invested by the Mahdists. She and her
fellow gunboats did what they could to pound enemy positions near the
river, and to weaken the enemy's stranglehold on the city.

AUTHOR'S NOTE

All images in this book are courtesy of the Stratford Archive, unless noted
otherwise

CONTENTS

NILE RIVER GUNBOATS 1882–1918

INTRODUCTION

During the later reign of Queen Victoria, gunboats played a key role in securing Britain's control of the north-eastern corner of Africa. They participated in every significant colonial campaign in the region, from the British invasion of Egypt in 1882 to the battle of Omdurman in 1898, when Britain finally won back control of the Sudan. After that, the river gunboats helped maintain British control over both Egypt and the Sudan, and played a key role in safeguarding British interests around the headwaters of the Nile – a region hotly contested by several European powers. Although their heyday came during the two Sudanese campaigns of 1884–85 and 1898, these gunboats also patrolled the Red Sea from 1908 to 1918, and during World War I they enjoyed a last swansong, defending Egypt from the Ottoman Turks. For more than 30 years the Nile river gunboat was an indispensible tool of empire, policing the great river and acting as floating symbols of British imperial power. Even today these strange little vessels remain potent historical symbols of the 'Age of Empire'.

The gunboat *El Teb*, one of four in her class, being hauled through the rapids of the Fourth Cataract, 1898. While two teams drag her forward with ropes, two more on each bank haul equally hard to prevent her from veering towards the rocks on either side. Meanwhile, more soldiers holding spars stand by to fend her off if she gets too close to any smaller rocks.

Today, they are best remembered for their role in the two sweeping Victorian campaigns that played out in the sands of the Sudan. In 1884 they helped defend Khartoum against a vastly superior Mahdist army, and then they joined the brave but ultimately doomed British attempt to relieve the city, and save the life of General Gordon. In fact, their presence on the river Nile was the potential key to victory. The campaign might have ended differently if better use had been made both of them, and the river they operated on. One of the most dramatic episodes of the campaign was 'The River Dash' – an 11th-hour attempt to break through to Khartoum, and to rescue Gordon. The gunboats played a key part in this venture, and although they arrived too late to save the day, their gallant attempt caught the imagination of the Victorian public.

In 1896, the Nile gunboats returned to the Sudan. These initial operations were designed to provide a secure base on the river for a larger-scale invasion of the region, and its reconquest. This time the gunboats were better designed and in some cases tailor-made for the job. So, despite a few minor setbacks the river gunboats performed splendidly, and went on to spearhead the advance in 1898 that would ultimately lead to the battle of Omdurman, the recapture of Khartoum, and the subjugation of the Sudan. Then, although the glory days of these gunboats had passed, they continued to patrol the river, take part in punitive expeditions, and 'show the flag' in the face of colonial expansion by other European powers. Strangely, although the era of the Nile gunboats has long passed into history, two of them remain in Khartoum – gently decaying reminders of the splendour of Britain's imperial heyday. This book is dedicated to them, in the hope that it might kindle interest in their preservation.

THE RIVER

Long before the British arrived in the region the river Nile was patrolled by warships – Egyptian,

The 'Gunboat Station' at Khartoum, the steamer mooring in front of the Governor's House. The photo was taken in late 1889 or early 1900, after the final defeat of the remnants of the Mahdist army at Um Dibaykarat. Rather than formal jetties, the gunboats and transports were berthed alongside the shore, and accessed by a gangplank.

Ptolemaic, Byzantine, Turkish, and then Coptic again. This was understandable, as the Nile was more than just a great body of water. It was a strategic resource, and by controlling it, the states that maintained this naval presence could also ensure control of every aspect of life for those who lived along its banks. The Egyptian government of the late 19th century was perfectly aware of the river's importance, both to their own state and to their southern neighbours, the Sudanese. The Egyptians, and the British who eventually supplanted them, would not only continue this tradition of using warships to control the river, but they would do so by taking advantage of all the latest technology Victorian Britain had to offer.

The river was what provided life not only to Egypt, but also to its wilder southern neighbour. The Sudan was an inhospitable region, where settlements clustered along the great river. Control of its waters ultimately led to control of the whole country. The importance of the river to the Sudan was described with great clarity by Winston Churchill in *The River War*, his history of the 1898 campaign:

> The north-east corner of the continent of Africa is drained and watered by the Nile. Among and about the headstreams and tributaries of this mighty river lie the wide and fertile provinces of the Egyptian Sudan. Situated in the very centre of the land, these remote regions are on every side divided from the seas by 500 miles of mountain, swamp or desert. The great river is their only means of growth, their only channel of progress. It is by the Nile alone that their commerce can reach its outer markets, or European civilization can penetrate the inner darkness. The Sudan is joined to Egypt by the Nile, as a diver is connected to the surface by his air pipe. Without it there is only suffocation.

The Nile certainly was not an easy river to navigate. There were five cataracts between the Egyptian frontier and Khartoum, and crossing them required vessels to be lightened, and then dragged cautiously forward, taking great care to avoid the numerous rocks and shoals. Here, the passage of the Fourth Cataract is being undertaken by some of the small whalers which Major-General Wolseley hoped to use to transport much of his force upriver. They proved a disappointment.

Churchill went on to describe how the city of Khartoum, at the confluence of the White and Blue Niles, was a trading centre of great importance. It was the terminus both for the river trade from the north and the caravan trade routes from the south. To the south the two branches of the Nile became more fertile as they headed upstream towards Equatorial Africa. However, from their confluence at Khartoum, the river wound its way towards the north for 1,200 miles towards Aswan, beyond the Egyptian frontier. The landscape through which it passed was bleak – for the most part a barren desert, interspersed by ranges of low crags and clumps of black rock. Then, as Churchill put it: 'At last the wilderness recedes, and the living world broadens out again into Egypt and the Delta.' In other words, from the Egyptian border to Khartoum, the river Nile was the only viable means of transport, without enduring all the hardship involved in a trek across the desert under a blazing sun.

The river gunboat *Safia* approaching the island of Mernat in the Nile opposite Wad Hamed, where in February 1885 Colonel Sir Charles Wilson established a fortified encampment, 40 miles upriver from Gubat. Wilson's gunboats had tried to break through to Khartoum, but the city had fallen by the time the vessels arrived there. This engraving was published in the *Illustrated London News* in 1885.

The Nile has one significant tributary in this stretch – the river Atbara, which runs off towards the south-east for 500 miles. Also, the river is not straight, but between Wadi Halfa on the Egyptian frontier and Khartoum it forms a giant 'S', as it weaves between the craggy hills of the Dongola region. This means that at one point the distance across the desert from Korti to Metemmeh is just over 150 miles, while by river the distance is twice that.

Then there are the cataracts, where the river grows shallow, and runs fast between rocks. There are six of them, five of which are between Wadi Halfa and Khartoum. Crossing them in small craft is difficult. It is much more so in a large gunboat, however shallow its draught might be. They were also seasonal, and for much of the spring and summer many were completely impassable. In other words, while having a naval

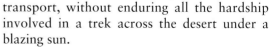

presence at Khartoum would allow these warships to control this vital stretch of life-giving river, the practical challenges involved in reaching Khartoum in the first place were significant.

British interests on the Nile

In 1869 the first ship – a British liner – passed through the Suez Canal, and the nature of north-eastern Africa was changed forever. The new canal was a strategic resource of the greatest importance, and this was particularly true for Britain, for which it dramatically reduced the journey time to India. When the Egyptian Khedive was ousted in a military coup in 1879, British intervention in the region became inevitable, in order to protect its newfound strategic interests. The invasion began in 1882 with a naval bombardment of Alexandria. Troops were landed, and within a month the Egyptian army was soundly defeated at the battle of Tel-el-Kebir. Power was restored to the pro-British Khedive, and from then on, while the country remained Egyptian, it was ruled with British 'assistance'.

Since 1819, the Sudan had been ruled by the Egyptians. In 1873, the Khedive appointed General Charles Gordon as his governor in the Sudan. He saw it as his moral duty to oppose the slave trade, and when the Khedive was ousted he lost the support he needed to continue his efforts. So, he resigned in 1880, and returned to Britain. During his tenure as governor he realized the importance of controlling the waters of the Nile, and supervised the establishment of a small gunboat squadron at Khartoum. These vessels were not purpose-built as gunboats, but they were more than sufficient for the low-level threat posed at the time. That though, would change dramatically following the rise of the Mahdi, a Sudanese religious rebel. The destruction of the Hicks Expedition in 1883 gave the Mahdi's followers access to both modern Remington rifles and artillery, and the Egyptian government's Khartoum-based gunboats would now face far more deadly firepower as they fought to maintain Khartoum's river links with the outside world.

At the re-installed Khedive's request Gordon returned to Khartoum in February 1884, and set about improving the defences of the city. The following month the Sudanese tribes to the north of Khartoum rose in support of the Mahdi, thereby placing his lines of communication in jeopardy. Now his gunboat patrols came under fire from what had recently been friendly riverside settlements. Then, on 13 March the Mahdi's army arrived, and invested the city. One of the Mahdi's first

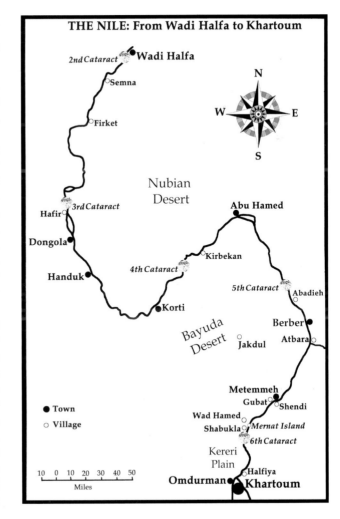

THE NILE: From Wadi Halfa to Khartoum

The Egyptian government's elegant sidewheel steamer *Bordein* on patrol near Khartoum, 1883. She was built in London for the Nile expedition of 1871, and shipped east in pieces, to be reassembled in Cairo. She took part in both the Hicks Expedition of 1883, and the Siege of Khartoum the following year, until she ran aground on Mernat Island in January 1885.

acts was to place gun batteries overlooking the river, to prevent any breakout from Khartoum. Although the gunboats did what they could to keep this vital artery open, it soon became clear that Khartoum was cut off from the outside world. A gunboat made it down the river though – or at least its passengers and crew did – and when their news of the situation reached Britain the public demanded action. So, an expedition was sent to relieve Khartoum, and to rescue Gordon. The scene was set for what would be the first real test of the Nile river gunboat.

NILE GUNBOAT DEVELOPMENT

General Gordon's 'Penny Steamers'

None of the gunboats at Gordon's disposal at Khartoum in 1884 were purpose-built warships. Instead they were civilian steamers, bought into service by the Egyptian government to carry mail and passengers on the Upper Nile. They were armed with what limited weaponry was available, and protected by whatever lay to hand. For the most part this involved protecting their upper works with heavy baulks of timber, leaving embrasures in them to accommodate the French 9-pdr howitzers or 90mm Krupp field guns Gordon had mounted in them. Additional protection was provided by metal plates, and sandbags. This gave these vessels a somewhat rustic appearance, a little like a floating wooden stockade.

If available, additional weaponry such as Nordenfelt or Gardner machine guns was also installed in the vessels. These ships were dubbed Gordon's 'penny steamers', after the small passenger steamers of the time. They all had a fairly similar appearance: they were sidewheel steamers, with a pair of paddleboxes amidships, and boasted a tall, thin funnel further astern. All of them were fairly narrow-beamed, which gave them a fast, elegant appearance, and they usually had an open steering position or bridge – either a flying bridge spanning the paddlewheel boxes, or a smaller rectangular steering position further aft, on the roof of the after superstructure. While reasonably fast and manoeuvrable, they were poorly designed for service on the Upper Nile, and as gunboats their makeshift armament and protection was less than ideal.

One of the largest of these 'penny steamers' was the *Bordein*. Built in Poplar in 1869, she was originally ordered by Sir Samuel Baker for use in his Nile Expedition of 1871. She was built in kit form, shipped to Egypt, then assembled in the Boulak Dockyard in Cairo during 1870. While his expedition combined the suppression of slavery with exploration, the *Bordein* was still unarmed when Baker returned to Britain in 1873, and the steamer was bought into service by the Egyptian government. Three other steamers – the *Safīa*, the *Mansoura* and the *Talahawiyeh* – were of broadly similar construction, and were used in a civil capacity on the Upper Nile. In fact the *Talahawiyeh* was built in the same Poplar shipyard as the *Bordein*, but was 30ft longer, and had a slightly wider beam. All of them, if not already serving in that capacity, were pressed into service as gunboats by Gordon in early 1884. In addition there were several other smaller steamers, some of which were lightly armed, but cannot with any justification be described as gunboats.

The *Bordein*, the *Safīa* and the *Talahawiyeh*, together with two smaller steamers, were all ordered to break through the Mahdist defences, and to rendezvous with the relief column advancing from the Egyptian frontier. Of these, the *Bordein* and the *Talahawiyeh* returned to Khartoum in 'The River Dash', but arrived too late to save the city. During this operation and its aftermath both vessels were wrecked, and subsequently refloated and repaired by the Mahdists.

Tamai-class gunboats

Meanwhile, a class of four gunboats was being built for service on the Nile. They were ordered in late 1884, the contract approved by the British Admiralty acting on behalf of the Egyptian government. The vessels took the best part of a year to design, and so were only built in 1886, after the Sudan campaign of 1884–85 had come to an end. They were built on the Clyde, at the Fairfield shipyard in Govan, and unlike the 'penny steamers' that drew more water, these craft were designed to have a draught of just 2ft 6in when fully laden. They were also sternwheelers, which were considered better able to cope with the vagaries of the river than sidewheelers were.

The powerful sternwheel gunboat *El Zafir* engaging the Mahdist-held fort at Shendi, on the eastern bank of the Nile, a few miles downriver from Metemmeh. She was one of the gunboats that arrived there in October 1897, as part of a three-vessel flotilla that spent three days subduing the fort.

On reaching Omdurman on 1 September 1898, while the army disembarked above the city, the gunboats steamed upriver to engage the Mahdist positions there. In this engraving, the gunboat *Sultan* is shown in action against Mahdist defences beneath the Mahdi's tomb.

These four boats were built in 1886, and shipped east in pieces, to be reassembled in Cairo. The *Tamai* and her sisters *Abu Klea*, *Metemmeh* and *El Teb* (later renamed *Hafir*) were duly used to patrol Egyptian waters, and to prepare for the British return to the Sudan – a campaign of reconquest demanded by the British public to avenge the death of Gordon.

El Zafir-class gunboats

A new batch of slightly larger vessels was ordered in 1895, when plans were being laid for the Dongola Campaign – a limited invasion of the northern Sudan, aimed at establishing a British forward base on the Nile above the Fifth Cataract. Like the earlier Tamai-class gunboats, these three El Zafir-class vessels would be sternwheelers, but larger than their predecessors, and better armed. With more ordnance aboard they drew a little more water (2ft 9in rather than 2ft 6in when fully laden), but their extra firepower was considered vital if the gunboat flotilla was to subdue Mahdist fortifications, particularly the substantial Egyptian-built fort overlooking the Upper Nile at Shendi. Like their predecessors, these were designed and built in Britain, and then shipped east. The El Zafir-class vessels were however then taken up the Nile, and reassembled above the Second Cataract. Earlier experience suggested that it was wisest to mount the vessels' heavy guns as high in the superstructure as possible, to give the best possible field of fire. This was particularly important as many Mahdist gun positions were dug in, making them difficult to hit effectively from ordnance mounted at deck level. In fact the three 'large sternwheelers' *El Zafir*, *El Nasir* and *El Fateh* arrived on the Upper Nile too late to participate in the opening battles of the Dongola Campaign of 1896, and were reduced to a supporting role during the subsequent mopping-up operations. However, all three would play an important part in the larger-scale campaign of 1897–98.

Sultan-class gunboats

In 1896, the Admiralty ordered a new trio of powerful gunboats for service on the Upper Nile; again, the order was by the Admiralty on behalf of the Egyptian government. Their design was based on the experience gained during the 1884–85 Sudan campaign, and from the more tangible evidence supplied by the performance of the Tamai-class gunboats on the Lower Nile over the subsequent decade. The result was a vessel which was as close to perfectly designed for the Upper Nile as possible. These craft would have a low freeboard, but a reasonably wide beam, to accommodate troops and stores. Vulnerable paddlewheel boxes were replaced by screw propellers, mounted in recessed grooves in the underside of the hull, to reduce the risk of damage from grounding or underwater obstructions. This gave them a decent maximum speed of 12 knots. They had reasonable

The gunboat *Melik* in action on 1 September 1898, followed by her two sister ships *Sultan* and *Sheikh*. They are shown steaming upriver between two hostile shores – Omdurman on their port side, and Tuti Island to starboard. *Melik* is depicted engaging the Mahdist defences near the Mahdi's tomb, on the western shore.

standards of accommodation, and above all they were well armed.

Each was designed to carry two 12-pdr (3in) guns, mounted in the superstructure where they had a good field of fire. These were augmented by a battery of six Maxim machine guns, most of which were mounted on a battery deck behind the funnel. Finally they were designed to carry two 5in howitzers, on field carriages, crewed by Egyptian army gunners. Otherwise, a mix of Royal Naval, Royal Marine and Egyptian gunners were to be employed. The vessels were built in two small shipyards on the river Thames, and built quickly, thanks to the Admiralty's close supervision. After all, with a campaign of reconquest planned in the Sudan, these ships would be vital. It could even be argued that the success of Kitchener's forthcoming campaign depended on them.

The three gunboats were completed in 1897, then dismantled into carefully marked sections. The components were transported by ship to the Suez Canal, where they were transhipped onto river vessels and taken up the Ismailia Canal to the Nile, and on to Wadi Halfa. There the sections were

The gunboat *Sultan*, photographed around 1910, while serving off Khartoum. By this stage her after superstructure had been altered, so she lacked the high protective bulwarks in evidence during the 1898 campaign. The result is a cleaner, less cluttered appearance.

loaded onto railway wagons, and taken up the newly-built Desert Railway to Abadieh on the Nile, near Berber. There *Sultan*, *Sheikh* and *Melik* were reassembled, and launched into the waters of the Nile. While General Kitchener had his other gunboats – vessels of the Tamai and El Zafir classes – as well as a host of auxiliary vessels, these three powerful new gunboats were destined to form the spearhead of the British advance up the Upper Nile, and the campaign of revenge and conquest that would reach its climax with the battle of Omdurman.

THE NILE GUNBOATS

The small gunboats serving on the Upper Nile came in a variety of shapes and sizes, from the small 'penny steamers' used by Gordon to defend Khartoum to the larger purpose-built gunboats which were used during General Kitchener's 1898 campaign. While information on some of these – particularly the smaller gunboats – is somewhat patchy and sometimes contradictory, this catalogue represents a précis of what reliable details are available.

The 'Penny Steamers'

Bordein	
Built	Samuda Brothers Shipyard, Poplar, London, 1869. Reassembled at Boulak Dockyard, Cairo, 1870
Displacement	Unrecorded
Dimensions	Length: 140ft
	Beam: 12ft (26ft with paddleboxes)
	Draught: 3ft 6in
Propulsion	Twin paddlewheels, 40hp
Maximum speed	10 knots (although speed reportedly reduced to 5 knots by 1885)
Armament	Two 9-pdr rifled breech-loading guns
Operational summary	Built for Sir Samuel Baker's Expedition of 1871, and subsequently sold into Egyptian service at Khartoum. She took part in the Hicks Expedition of 1883, and subsequently participated in the defence of Khartoum. In early 1885 she escaped downriver to link up with the advancing British Army, and then took part in 'The River Dash'. On her return she was wrecked near Mernat Island on 31 January 1885. She was subsequently salvaged by the Mahdists, and remained in their hands until 1898, when she was recaptured off Omdurman. After that she was used as a local river transport until 1905. She was briefly restored in 1936–37, but then abandoned again. Her hull is still extant, in Khartoum.

1: *BORDEIN* (1884)

The *Bordein* was a sidewheel paddle steamer, built in Poplar in 1869, and which began service on the Nile in 1871. In 1883 she took part in Hicks Pasha's doomed expedition, and in 1885 took part in 'The River Dash', but ran aground near Mernat Island on 31 January 1885. Abandoned by her crew, she was subsequently refloated, and served under the Mahdi's banner. In this illustration she is shown patrolling the waters of the Nile off Gubat Island. Her bulwarks and superstructure have been reinforced by timber and sheet metal, while a 'pillbox' provides cover for her gunners on her forecastle.

2: *TAMAI* (1896)

The *Tamai* was a sternwheel gunboat, one of a class of four vessels. Her sister ships were the *Abu Klea, El Teb* and *Metemmeh*. These small sternwheelers were all built during the 1880s, and initially armed with a single 90mm Krupp gun forward, and two Nordenfelt machine guns, one covering each beam. They entered service too late to serve in the Gordon Relief Expedition, so they remained on the lower Nile until 1896. They were subsequently re-armed with 12-pdr (3in) guns, 1-pdr pom-poms and Maxim machine guns. The *Tamai*, named after the battle of 1884, served as the flagship of the gunboat squadron in 1896, and subsequently took part in the 1898 campaign.

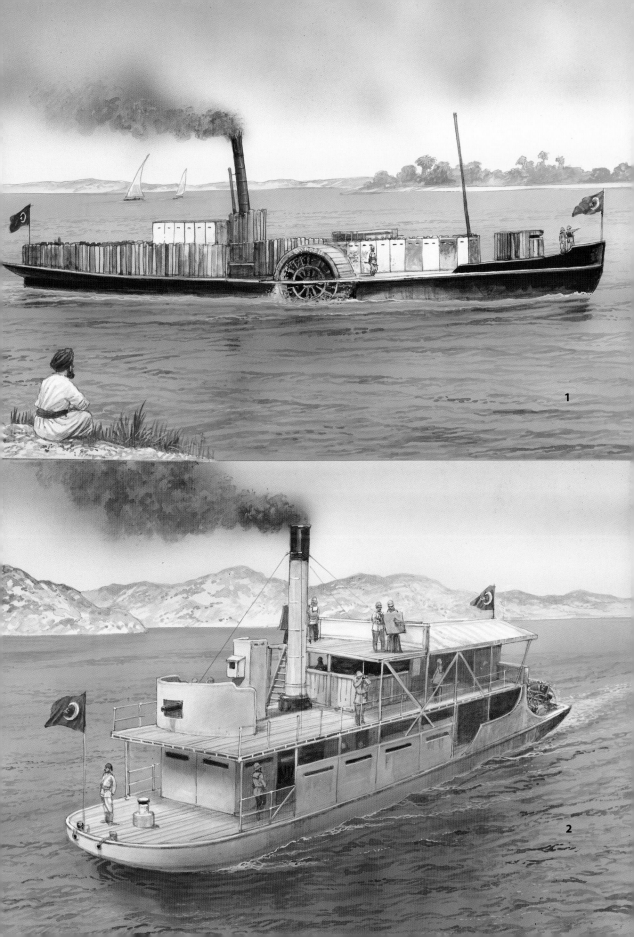

This photo of the gunboat *Bordein* was taken in 1936, soon after she was restored for the cancelled coronation of that year, after three decades of neglect. Behind her is the Governor's House in Khartoum. It is now the Presidential Palace.

Talahawiyeh (also known as *Tel El-Hoween*)	
Built	Samuda Brothers Shipyard, Poplar, London, 1868. Reassembled at Boulak Dockyard, Cairo, 1870
Displacement	Unrecorded
Dimensions	Length: 160ft
	Beam: 14ft (28ft with paddleboxes)
	Draught: 3ft 6in
Propulsion	Twin paddlewheels, 60hp
Maximum speed	10 knots (although speed reportedly reduced to 5 knots by 1885)
Armament	Two 9-pdr rifled breech-loading guns
Note	Possessed a large after cabin and saloon. A near-sister to the *Bordein*, but she was slightly larger
Operational summary	Built for Sir Samuel Baker's Expedition of 1871, and subsequently sold into Egyptian service at Khartoum. She took part in the Hicks Expedition of 1883, and subsequently sent by Gordon to Sheni to patrol the lower reaches of the Upper Nile. She participated in 'The River Dash' in January–February 1885, but was wrecked on the Jebel Royan at the Sixth Cataract on 29 January 1885. She was never raised, and her boiler could still be seen there as late as 1909.

The Tamai-class gunboats had an armoured wheelhouse and conning tower in front of the funnel, and a substantial semi-circular fixed gunshield forward. This extended to the main deck, in the form of a loopholed steel pillbox, while the vessel's steel-clad bulwarks also offered protection against enemy small-arms fire. This vessel is probably the *Metemmeh*.

Safia

Built	Samuda Brothers Shipyard, Poplar, London, 1870. Reassembled at Boulak Dockyard, Cairo, 1871
Displacement	Unrecorded
Dimensions	Length: 135ft
	Beam: 11ft (25ft with paddleboxes)
	Draught: 3ft 6in
Propulsion	Twin paddlewheels, 50hp
Maximum speed	8 knots
Armament	Two 9-pdr rifled breech-loading guns, two Gardner machine guns
Operational summary	Built for Sir Samuel Baker's Expedition of 1871, but used to run dispatches and as an administration vessel for two decades, first by Baker, and then by Gordon. In September 1880 she ran out of fuel and was stranded in the barren Sudd swamps on the Bahr el Ghazal river in southern Sudan. By the time a relief force reached her in the *Bordein* four months later most of her crew had died of starvation or disease. Some, according to the reports, had also resorted to cannibalism. She took part in the Hicks Expedition of 1883, and the following year was sent downstream to Shendi. Although she didn't participate in 'The River Dash', in early February 1885 she was called upon to rescue the crew of the stranded *Bordein* from Mernat Island, while under heavy fire. She was disabled for a time, but managed to escape when her boiler was patched. She took such a hammering that she was eventually scuttled off Gerbat on 13 February 1885. However, she was subsequently salvaged by the Mahdists, and remained in their hands until 15 September 1898, when she was recaptured by the gunboat *Sultan* after a brief exchange of fire. She was repaired, and sent to Fashoda later in 1898, in support of British forces there. She remained in service until 1905, when her engines were removed and she became a cargo lighter. She was disposed of sometime after 1912.

Tawfiqiyeh

Built	London, 1873. Reassembled in Cairo, 1875
Displacement	Unrecorded
Dimensions	Length: 110ft
	Beam: 10ft 6in (21ft with paddleboxes)
	Draught: 2ft 6in
Propulsion	Twin paddlewheels, 40hp
Maximum speed	8 knots
Armament	Unknown, but probably one 90mm Krupp field gun and one 4-pdr muzzle-loading mountain gun, both on field carriages
Operational summary	Built for Egyptian government service on the Upper Nile, the vessel was stationed at Shendi for much of her brief life. In 1883–84 she remained patrolling the Nile between Shendi and Khartoum, and after linking up with the advancing British River Column, she operated in support of it throughout 1885. She was almost certainly scuttled off Gerbat on 13 February 1885. There is no evidence that she was subsequently salvaged.

Mansoura (also known as the *Mansurah*)

Built	Samuda Brothers Shipyard, Poplar, London, 1870. Reassembled at Boulak Dockyard, Cairo, 1871
Displacement	Unrecorded
Dimensions	Length 140ft
	Beam: 12ft 6in (25ft 6in with paddleboxes)
	Draught: 4ft
Propulsion	Twin paddlewheels, 50hp
Maximum speed	9 knots
Armament	Unknown, but probably one 90mm Krupp field gun, and one 4-pdr muzzle-loading mountain gun, both on field carriages
Operational summary	Built for Sir Samuel Baker's Expedition of 1871, but saw no service with him. Instead she was used by the Egyptian government as a mail steamer, and then pressed into service by Gordon as a makeshift gunboat. She operated in support of the Hicks Expedition of 1883, and in 1884 Gordon sent her downriver to Shendi, to protect his lines of communication back to Khartoum. She was holed below the waterline by fire from a Mahdist battery at Miseiktab, a few miles north of Shendi on 7 December 1884, and sank in mid-river during the night.

Other Khartoum gunboats

Two other gunboats formed part of the flotilla at Khartoum. The *Shebeen* (or *Shibi*) and the *Embara* were both slightly smaller versions of the *Bordein*, used by the Egyptian government as despatch vessels, and based at Khartoum. They were employed during the ill-fated Hicks Expedition of 1883, but the

The government gunboat *Abbās* escaped down the Nile from besieged Khartoum, only to run aground on 18 September 1884, near the village of Hebbeh. Although her passengers and crew reached safety, the gunboat was completely wrecked. This sketch of her appeared in the *Graphic Illustrated* journal of November 1884.

Embara was wrecked at Al Wan near the Sixth Cataract later that year. The *Shebeen* was undergoing much-needed repairs in Khartoum in early 1884, and she remained out of the water there until the fall of the city. She was subsequently dismantled by the Mahdists and used for spares to keep their fleet of captured gunboats operational. Both were sidewheel steamers. The *Ismaileih* and the *Abbās* were small sidewheel steamers in Egyptian employment, and largely used to transport passengers. Both were smaller than the other 'penny-packet' steamers, and although both were armed by Gordon, there appears to be no record of their armament.

Later gunboats

Tamai-class (*Tamai*, *Abu Klea*, *El Teb* and *Metemmeh*)

Note	Often referred to as 'small sternwheel gunboats'
Built	1884–85. *Tamai* and *El Teb* by Randolph, Elder & Co., Clydeside (renamed Fairfield Shipbuilding in 1886); *Abu Klea* and *Metemmeh* by Yarrow & Co., Poplar, London. Assembled in Cairo 1885–86
Displacement	73.5 tons
Dimensions	Length: 89ft
	Beam: 18ft
	Draught: 1ft 6in (2ft 6in when laden)
Propulsion	A stern paddlewheel, 50hp
Maximum speed	9 knots
Armament	One 12-pdr (3in) QF gun Mark I, two 1-pdr pom-poms, and four Maxim machine guns. Before 1894, these gunboats were armed with one 90mm Krupp field gun and two Nordenfelt machine guns
Operational summaries	Tamai-class entered service in 1886. Patrolled Lower Nile until Dongola campaign of 1896. *Tamai*, *Abu Klea* and *Metemmeh* participated in the bombardment of Hafir (September 1896), forcing Mahdists to withdraw. *El Teb* renamed *Hafir* in 1897. Bombarded other Mahdist positions at Metemmeh (1897), and subsequently involved in bombardment and capture of Shendi, then the battle of Omdurman and the recapture of Khartoum (1898). *Metemmeh* underwent refit and modernization in Cairo in 1911, and all four modernized in 1921–25.
Fates	*Tamai* wrecked in the Red Sea, 1915
	Abu Klea scrapped in 1937
	El Teb/*Hafir* sunk accidentally in 1941
	Metemmeh decommissioned in 1925, and last recorded in 1964

El Zafir-class (*El Zafir, El Nasir* and *El Fateh*)

Note	Often referred to as 'large sternwheel gunboats'. In Arabic, *Zafir* means 'Victorious', *Fateh* 'Conqueror' and *Nasir* 'Majestic'
Built	1895, by Rennie Forest, Wivenhoe, Essex. Assembled in Cairo 1896
Displacement	128 tons
Dimensions	Length: 128ft
	Beam: 23ft
	Draught: 2ft
Propulsion	A stern paddlewheel, 90shp
Maximum speed	11 knots
Armament	One 12-pdr (3in) QF gun Mark I, one Hotchkiss 1-pdr, two to four Maxim machine guns
Operational summaries	El Zafir-class entered service 1896–97, and saw service during the Dongola campaign. In 1898 all three gunboats were involved in the bombardment and capture of Shendi, the battle of Omdurman and the recapture of Khartoum. *El Fateh* and *El Nasir* involved in the Fashoda Incident (1898). *El Nasir* modernized in 1915 for service in the Red Sea.
Fates	*El Zafir* sunk by accident off Shendi, 22 August 1898. Raised, repaired and returned to service the following year. Finally broken up 1964.
	El Fateh decommissioned and sold from service in 1925, and subsequently operated as a Nile passenger ferry. Finally broken up in 1953. *El Nasir* foundered on the Upper Nile in 1931. Although raised, she was decommissioned and broken up the following year.

Sultan-class (*Sultan, Sheikh* and *Melik*)

Note	Often referred to as 'twin-screw gunboats'
Built	1896. *Sultan* and *Sheik* by Yarrow & Co., Poplar, London; *Melik* by John I. Thorneycroft, Chiswick. Assembled in Abadiyah on Upper Nile, 1898
Displacement	134 tons
Dimensions	Length: 145ft
	Beam: 24ft 6in
	Draught: 2ft (2ft 6in when fully laden)
Propulsion	Two steam engines, powering two propellers, 200shp
Maximum speed	12 knots
Armament	Two 12-pdr (3in) QF guns Mark I, six Maxim machine guns
Operational summaries	Sultan-class vessels all participated in the 1898 campaign, and saw action off Omdurman, and in the recapture of Khartoum. *Sultan* participated in the Fashoda Incident later that year. Used as patrol vessels on the Upper Nile until 1925. *Melik* recommissioned in 1939–46, and served as a transport vessel for the Sudan Defence force, carrying oil drums. She was returned to her owners after the war.
Fates	All three gunboats decommissioned and sold out of service in 1925. *Sultan* used by Dorman Long construction company, and scuttled as breakwater during construction of Omdurman Bridge. Disarmed, *Sheikh* became the floating headquarters of the Khartoum Yacht Club, and *Melik* the headquarters of the Blue Nile Sailing Club. *Melik* used for filming *The Four Feathers* in 1939, then recommissioned the following year. Served as a wartime transport vessel. Decommissioned again in 1946. Returned to sailing club, and although removed from the water in 1987, she is still extant in Khartoum. The Melik Society hopes to preserve her as a historic vessel.

The Sultan-class gunboat *Sheikh*, pictured around 1910, by which time she had been repainted with a white hull and superstructure, and a buff-coloured funnel. Like her two sister ships she remained a regular sight on the Nile until after World War I.

Protection

General Gordon's 'penny packet' flotilla was made up of completely unprotected sidewheel steamers, most of which were pressed into service as makeshift gunboats. This meant they had to be given protection as well as some form of armament, using whatever lay to hand in Khartoum – baulks of timber, sheets of plate metal, and home-made sandbags. The following description by Colonel Sir Charles Wilson describes just how rudimentary this protection was. He embarked on the *Bordein* for 'The River Dash', but the gunboat's consort *Talahawiyeh* was protected in a virtually identical way:

> The two boats were fitted in much the same way. At the bow a small space was left for the cable, and then came a rude turret of baulks of wood fastened together with iron pins, and built up from the deck so as to give a gun platform to fire over the bulwarks. The turret was not round, but spay-shaped, to fit the bows. It was bullet-proof, but not shot or shell-proof, and it was open at top. In this turret there was one gun firing right through the port-hole… Behind this was the hatchway of the fore hold, and a gangway on each side for landing; then the foremast, to which a bird-cage was slung for a lookout man – a sort of iron bucket. Next followed on each side small dirty cabins at either end of the paddleboxes – and between the paddleboxes and the midships turret – a square box, built, like the other, of baulks of wood pinned together.
>
> The floor of the turret was just high enough to enable the one gun to fire well over the top of the paddle-boxes. It had a port on each side, and was reached from the after part of the ship by a ladder which led to a small square hole, through which it took a moment to squeeze one's self. From the ports one could get out on top of the paddle boxes. Thus, anyone going to the turret in action was unpleasantly exposed. Within the turret, shot, shell and cartridges were lying about in a way that would soon have put an end to a boat not manned by Orientals. After the turret came the funnel, with many a bullet hole through it, and the boiler, partly above deck and protected by logs of wood placed over it. Then came the hatchway of the main hold, and just behind it a saloon or deck house, a slight wooden structure divided into two rooms, and having a narrow passage running round it.

The gunboat *Safia*, returning to Gubat under enemy fire, after the rescue of Sir Charles Wilson and his men, February 1885.

In this stirring engraving by the war artist Richard Caton Woodville for the *Illustrated London News*, an Egyptian government steamer uses its bow-mounted Krupp field gun to engage Mahdists on the riverbank during one of the Khartoum flotilla's many sorties in defence of the city in late 1884.

On top of the saloon a place had been prepared for infantry, by making walls of boiler-plate iron, except at the entrance. The wheel was on the top of this deckhouse, and particular care had been taken to protect the helmsmen as much as possible. Behind the deckhouse was a little open space in the stern, with a hatchway leading to a small hold.

Round the sides of the ship the bulwarks and deckhouse were protected by sheets of boiler-plate fixed to wooden stanchions, except where the cabins and paddle-boxes came. The plates were just high enough to allow a man to fire over them, and along the top of the stanchions ran a wooden beam sufficiently raised above the plates to leave a long loophole. This gave excellent cover, and was bulletproof, except at ranges under 150 yards. To shot and shell it offered no protection, and unfortunately it was broken in several places, especially at the stern, where some sheets had disappeared. It also left about 1ft of the upper portion of the deckhouse quite exposed.

Wilson also stated that the *Safia* and *Tawfiqiyeh* – the other two gunboats in the 'penny packet' flotilla that ran down to rendezvous with the relief column – were protected in a similar manner. We can assume that the *Mansoura* was similarly protected. This is confirmed by the following description by Captain Lord Charles Beresford RN of the steamer *Safia*:

> In the bows was a small turret constructed of baulks of timber and containing a 9-pounder brass howitzer to fire ahead. Amidships, between the paddleboxes, was the central turret, also built of timber and mounting a gun to fire over the paddleboxes. Astern, on the roof of the deckhouse, was an enclosure of boiler plate, above which was fixed a rail of thick timber, leaving some space through which to fire. The boiler, which was protected above the deck, was jacketed with logs of wood.

One of the most telling parts of Wilson's description is his estimate that this protection was effective against Mahdist small-arms fire at ranges of more than 150 yards. Some stretches of the river between Metemmeh and Khartoum

This watercolour by Captain Willoughby Verner shows the Naval Brigade soldiers embarked on a gunboat in action in early 1885. Note the use of boiler plates to provide cover on the starboard side, while much of the bulwark on the port side is only protected by planking. This emphasises the pragmatic way in which these ships were protected, making the best use of the limited metal sheeting available – most of the enemy defences were reportedly on the river's western bank.

were 600–800 yards wide, which meant that steamers in the middle of the channel were reasonably well-protected. In many other places though, the numerous islands or choke-points in the river meant that a steamer running the gauntlet of fire from both banks would be dangerously exposed. Also, thanks to the shifting sandbanks and other obstacles, the *reis* or pilot could not always choose the safe course in the middle of the river, but had to follow a deeper channel, which might run closer to one of the banks.

The experience gained operating gunboats on the Upper Nile in 1884–85 led to the next generation of vessels being built with a more adequate degree of protection. Both the Tamai-class and El Zafir-class of gunboats had 1–1½in of steel plating over their most vulnerable spaces: the cylindrical wheelhouse and conning tower, and the boiler space. In addition, a protective bulwark of 1in-thick metal plate ran around the lower deck, providing a reasonably secure firing position for soldiers embarked on the vessels. Strangely the gun positions were more exposed, in most cases only the gunshields of the weapons themselves – 12-pdrs, 1-pdr 'pom-poms' or machine guns – offering the crew any real protection. However, the main gun position forward was protected by a fixed semi-circular screen. So, during the 1896 Dongola campaign, and again

B

1: *SAFĪA* (1885)

In 1883 the *Safia* was one of the Egyptian government's Khartoum-based sidewheel gunboats. She was a similar vessel to the *Bordein* – a near-sister, although she was slightly smaller. In 1884 she was heavily altered by adding crude wooden shuttering to provide protection for her Egyptian crew. Brass 9-pdr howitzers were mounted in her bow and stern, and Gardner machine guns were fitted amidships. After escaping from Khartoum she joined forces with the Gordon Relief Expedition, and under the command of Captain Lord Charles Beresford she saw action north of Gubat, but ran aground during the withdrawal to the Egyptian frontier. She was recaptured by the Mahdists, who operated her until 1898.

2: *EL ZAFIR* (1898)

The *El Zafir*, *El Fateh* and *El Nasir* were sister ships, built in Britain and shipped to the Nile for the 1898 expedition. These sternwheelers were larger than the sternwheelers of the Tamai-class, but notably smaller than the more modern screw gunboats of the Sultan-class. They were built for the 1896 campaign, but arrived too late to take part in much of it. So, their true baptism of fire came in 1898. Then, their substantial armament and manoeuvrability made them useful members of the gunboat flotilla. This plate shows the *El Zafir* as she looked during the latter stages of the 1898 campaign, where she saw extensive action off Shendi and Omdurman.

1

2

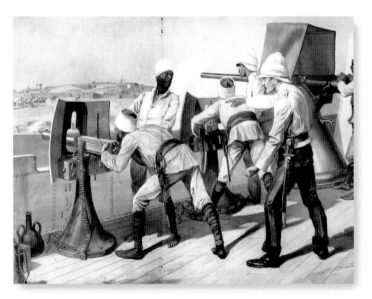

The starboard side of the gun deck of a Sultan-class gunboat, engaging Mahdist positions above Metemmeh during Kitchener's advance up the Nile to Mernat Island and Wad Hamed in August 1898. A Maxim machine gun and a 12-pdr can be seen engaging the Mahdists on the river bank.

in 1897–98, the defences appear to have been augmented in places with sandbags.

The stern paddlewheel boxes remained exposed, and therefore vulnerable. No effective solution was found to render these less exposed, as to encase them in a protective screen would have added far too much weight to the stern. This would have dramatically increased their draught, and rendered them unsuitable for operations in the shallow waters of the Upper Nile. By contrast the gunboats of the Sultan-class were excellently protected, with 1½–2in steel plate used in their construction. While this still was not proof against enemy artillery fire, it offered sufficient protection for the men on board that the gunboat could operate close inshore if required, where its machine guns could be used to devastating effect. Effectively, the Sultan-class was immune to rifle fire, unless a crewman exposed himself needlessly. This rendered these small but powerful vessels very potent war machines during Kitchener's drive up the Nile to Khartoum.

Propulsion

The 'penny packet' gunboats were all propelled by sidewheel paddles. This was less than ideal in a gunboat, as the wheels were extremely vulnerable to enemy fire. On the *Bordein* for instance, each of these paddlewheel boxes was approximately 7ft (2.1m) wide, and formed great semi-circular arches above the upper deck, encased in a thin metal housing. Below the level of the upper deck and above the waterline the paddlewheel was completely exposed, and therefore vulnerable. One good hit from an enemy shell could disable one of the two wheels, and render the gunboat incapable of manoeuvring in the narrow river.

The makeshift gunboat (or armed steamer) *Nasaf El-Khaih* being hauled cautiously around rocks blocking the Nile at the Second Cataract, just above Wadi Halfa, late 1884. The difficulties encountered both here and at the Third Cataract during the advance on Korti made General Wolseley appreciate the real problems involved in using river transport during the relief attempt.

The boilers and engines themselves were also large and vulnerable, although their location almost between the paddleboxes offered them some degree of protection. Their real weakness was their lack of propulsive power.

These Nile sidewheel steamers were mostly powered by side-lever engines, with one engine powering each wheel. The 'side-lever' was merely the moving bar that linked the paddle shaft to the engine piston. The piston operated vertically inside a double-acting cylinder – one where power was generated on both the up and down strokes of the piston. A system of levers (known as 'parallel motion mechanisms') linked this to the side lever, and the side lever to the paddle shaft. The side levers themselves were fitted as low as possible in the engine space, at the foot of the cylinders. The engine was fairly self-contained, with a condenser, an air pump and a hotwell (sump). A valve directed steam from the boiler into and out of the cylinder.

Boilers were of the tubular-type, which meant the furnace was surmounted by a large iron dome, inside which the steam space was divided by a series of tubes, designed to increase the heating effect of the furnace. The trouble was that these were low-pressure boilers. As a result, the power generated by the engine was correspondingly low, and so speeds of less than 10 knots were the norm. The technology of these engines dated back to the 1860s, and marine propulsion had advanced considerably during the two decades since.

Their lack of power was not helped by a relatively poor level of maintenance. With the possible exception of the *Bordein* and the *Safîa*, which were regarded as fast vessels, by 1884–85 these 'penny steamers' were often incapable of making more than 5 knots, due to the loss of steam pressure, poorly fitting bearings and other mechanical defects. This was particularly true during the Siege of Khartoum, when these makeshift gunboats were in almost constant use, and there was little time for maintenance. However, Sir Charles Wilson noted that while the rest of these vessels might have been filthy, the engine spaces were not: 'The only part of the boats which had been well looked after were the engines which, though old and wanting a thorough overhauling, were clean and bright, and worked smoothly.'

The next generation of Nile gunboats, the sternwheelers, employed a far more modern system of propulsion. While their engines still powered a paddlewheel, albeit a large one at the stern, the engines themselves were double-expansion engines. These were compound engines, in which steam expanded in two stages – first a high-pressure stage, then a lower-pressure

The elegantly-proportioned sidewheel gunboat *Bordein* ran aground off Mernat Island below Khartoum, and was duly abandoned by her crew. She was subsequently refloated by the Mahdists, who used her themselves. She was eventually recaptured from them in 1898.

This 1885 artist's impression of a Tamai-class gunboat, produced for the *Illustrated London News*, shows just how exposed the engine and boilers initially were on these vessels. The tubular conning tower and the semi-circular fixed gunshield can also be clearly seen. By the time the Tamai-class vessels entered service, however, the engine spaces were protected by a metal housing, and the conning tower had been replaced by a more practical square structure.

one. The aim was to extract the maximum amount of power from the high-pressure steam injected into the engine, and they generated considerably more power than an earlier engine of the same size. In gunboats, this allowed the engines powering the sternwheel of the Tamai-class gunboats to be considerably smaller than the engines fitted to the older 'penny packet' steamers, but they generated more power. While this did not directly lead to a great increase in propulsive power or speed, it did mean that the engines were less bulky and more mechanically reliable.

The boilers of these purpose-built gunboats were also much better than those of their improvised predecessors. Still, these cylindrical boilers developed a reputation for being inconsistent in terms of their heating, which resulted in unwelcome fluctuations in steam pressure unless closely monitored. A new corrugated furnace had been developed in the late 1870s, but these were not fitted to the Tamai-class. Although *in extremis* these vessels could burn wood, they were designed to burn coal, which had to be shipped to the Upper Nile. While the older 'penny packet' steamers stopped now and again and demolished some huts to provide wood for their furnaces, the later gunboats all had to rely on regular coal shipments. This, among other things, was a deciding factor in Kitchener's decision to build a supply railway across the Nubian Desert, so that coal, ammunition, supplies and troops could all be transported quickly and easily from Egypt to the banks of the Upper Nile.

The Sultan-class gunboats employed the latest compact triple-expansion reciprocating engines, which were both efficient and extremely reliable. Unlike their predecessors though, these vessels were screw-powered, which rendered the vessels less vulnerable to enemy fire. As triple-expansion rather than double-expansion engines, these added a third cylinder where low pressure steam was passed, thereby providing an extra degree of power from the same initial injection of steam. The compact Scotch boilers fitted to these gunboats produced high-pressure steam, which could then be superheated to reduce loss during condensation. As a result these boilers could produce more power for the expenditure of less fuel – an important consideration in an area where supplies had to be imported, and where refuelling opportunities were often scarce. Apart from their reliance on imported fuel – a situation which was unavoidable – these gunboats were ideally designed for the Upper Nile, with the power to counter strong currents when required, and of course to steam into action with alacrity.

Conditions on board

General Gordon's flotilla of steamers flew the Egyptian flag, and for the most part were crewed by Africans. Colonel Sir Charles Wilson provides us with a colourful description of the gunboat crews he encountered during 'The River Dash':

Then the crews and soldiers were a most extraordinary lot. There was first of all the commandant, who was supposed to be in command of the soldiers and of the ship, and who really controlled the movements of the ship, and took command of the soldiers when they landed; the officer commanding the regulars – all blacks, once slaves; the officer commanding the artillery; the officer commanding the Shagiyeh [Shā iqīa] *bashi-bazouks* [irregulars]; Turkish bashi-bazouk officers, who had brought and commanded their own slaves; the captain who commanded the crew, which was split up into sections under their respective heads; the chief of the sailors; the chief of the caulkers, of the carpenters, the woodcutters etc.; the *Reis* or pilot with his assistants who navigated the ship; the helmsmen; the chief engineer with his assistants, and the stokers and firemen; and last, not least, the ladies who ground the dura into meal, and made the great wafer-like dura cakes in which the Sudanese delight.

The soldiers were all slaves, and the officers black, except those of the artillery, who were Egyptians. The Bashis were part Shagiyeh, partly black slaves, and partly half-caste; the officers of the Bashis were Turks, Kurds and Circassians, the captains and *reises* Dongolese, the sailors blacks and the engineers Egyptians. Such a motley crew, and such a business getting them to work together, or, in fact, to work at all, and as to the noise it was sometimes deafening. They were, however, a cheery, good-humoured lot, much like spoiled children, and quite amenable to King Kurbash [the whip]. Of course, when we got fairly underway, we found lots of men who ought not to have come – stowaways anxious to get up to their families, and wounded men who had concealed themselves above the bags of dura.

Muhammad Khashm al-Mūs Pasha, commander of the Sudanese irregular troops embarked on the Khartoum steamers during 'The River Dash'. When Khartoum fell his family were killed – a high price to pay for his steadfast loyalty to Gordon, and his support for the Egyptian government.

During 'The River Dash' of 1884–85, Wilson established himself in the *Bordein*, accompanied by his aide, Captain Frederick Gascoigne; Suleiman, his African manservant; his Royal Engineer batman; an Egyptian interpreter; a naval artificer to advise him in marine engineering; a sergeant; a lance-corporal; and eight soldiers of the Royal Sussex regiment. While he

A sailor of the Naval Brigade during the attempt to relieve Khartoum, 1884–85. In this watercolour by Willoughby Verner the seaman is shown wearing patched tropical whites, with boots, gaiters and a solar helmet. The three stripes on his sleeve indicate he is an experienced hand, with at least 12 years of service.

The careening of a river gunboat off Khartoum, c.1900. This was usually carried out on the opposite bank of the Blue Nile from the city, on Tuti Island. Blocks and tackles are used to winch the vessel out of the water and onto a makeshift slipway of wooden logs. Once out of the water the lower hull could be inspected, repaired if necessary, cleaned and repainted.

was effectively in command of both the *Bordein* and the accompanying *Talahawiyeh*, each ship had its own commander. In charge of the *Bordein* was Muhammad Khashm al-Mūs Pasha, the Melik (headman) of the Shā iqīa tribe of Nile Arabs, who, like his people, remained firmly loyal to the Egyptian government. Wilson described him as: 'a man of about 52 or 53, with greyish beard, rather short, not very beautiful, but with a certain amount of dignity.' Wilson added that he 'never does anything except sit on a sofa, whence he gives his orders, whilst smoking, and drinking coffee.'

Major-General Sir Garnet Wolseley examining a chart of the river Nile from his comfortable accommodation suite in the forward superstructure of his headquarters ship *Ferouz*. The ruins in the background suggest this engraving shows him off Wadi Halfa, on the border between Egypt and the Sudan. He planned to make as much use of the river as he could during his army's advance on Khartoum.

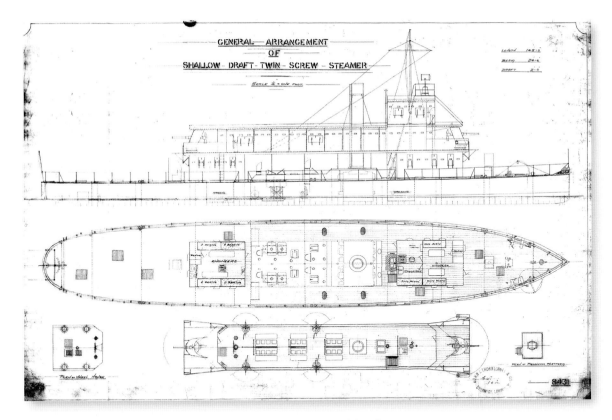

GENERAL — ARRANGEMENT
OF
SHALLOW — DRAFT — TWIN — SCREW — STEAMER

This appears a little unkind, as Khashm al-Mūs worked hard to motivate his troops, to ensure they were well-behaved when going ashore to collect wood to burn, and during the trials of the expedition's return from Khartoum, when the headman and his crew knew that the Mahdists had captured Khartoum, and even if their families had been spared, their chances of ever being reunited with them were slim. On the *Talahawiyeh* the senior British officer was Captain Lionel Trafford of the Royal Sussex regiment, supported by a lieutenant, a naval artificer and signaller, his batman, plus a corporal and nine soldiers from Trafford's regiment. On both gunboats the soldiers were all picked marksmen. The gunboat's commander was Abdul Hamid, another Shā iqīa leader, and a kinsman of Khashm. Wilson described him as 'a slight man' and 'very young – too young for the position he was holding.' He added that 'he had the petulant manners of a spoiled child.'

For 'The River Dash' this handful of British regulars and the native crews were augmented by 110–120 *bazingers* per ship – irregular soldiers of Sudanese descent in the service of the Egyptian government. Technically they were slaves, whose officers were also their overseers. They wore a semblance of a uniform, including a red fez. Wilson incorrectly described them as *bashi-bazouks*, who were irregular mercenaries, usually of Egyptian origin.

Wilson was equally dismissive of the condition he found the gunboats in. However, his description of their domestic arrangements is revealing:

> In the fore-hold was the gun and some of the rifle ammunition, with an enormous quantity of dura and loot, besides wood for the steamer. In the main hold were rifle ammunition, firewood, sacks of dura, bedding, loot of all kinds, women, a baby or two, and a herd of goats for milk. In the after hold were the loot and

The plans of a 'Shallow Draft Twin-Screw Steamer' – in this case the Sultan-class of three ships, *Sultan*, *Sheikh* and *Melik*. These plans show that despite her size her superstructure accommodation was not particularly roomy. What cabins there were were reserved for her British officers and senior non-commissioned officers. (The Melik Society)

Another watercolour by Captain Willoughby Verner showing a Nordenfelt machine gun in action on board a gunboat – probably the *Safia*. This ten-barrelled version of the weapon fired .45-calibre rounds, fed into the breeches from a ten-slot magazine. The sailor operated it by cranking the lever on the right-hand side of the stock.

property of the commandant. In fact every hole and corner below deck was filled with dura, Indian corn, fuel and loot, and on the deck we had as much dura as we could carry, piled up in sacks for the Khartoum garrison. What with these sacks and the large number of men on board, it was no easy matter getting about.

He also mentioned the cooking of these ubiquitous dura-cakes – a form of meal common in the Sudan:

They [the slave girls] are at it all day long – no rest. First the dura is ground between two stones... then the meal is mixed with water to the consistency of thick porridge; and lastly a great lump of it is thrown on a large circular iron dish heated by a wood-fire. With a little stick the girl dextrously manipulates the dough so that it covers the whole plate like a thin wafer; there is a noise of frying, and in a moment the finished cake is torn off ready for eating.

Less impressive to Wilson was the condition he found the ships in: 'The filth was something indescribable – the stench which rose up from the holds

C

1: *EL-KAIHAR*

The *Nasaf El-Kaihar* was a Nile sidewheel river steamer that was pressed into service in 1884 for the Gordon Relief Expedition. Built in the 1860s, she was given little in the way of extra protection or armament, as she served as the floating headquarters of Major-General Wolseley. Her only armament consisted of a pair of Nordenfelt machine guns, mounted just forward of her paddle wheels. Although not properly a gunboat, she is included here as a representative of the lightly armed auxiliary vessels which served in the expedition, either as patrol craft, transports or support vessels.

2: *SULTAN* (1898)

Having learned their lesson a decade before, before the reconquest of the Sudan was attempted a group of three purpose-built gunboats was ordered, to spearhead the expedition. The *Sultan* and her sisters *Melik* and *Sheik* were prefabricated in Britain, and then shipped out to Egypt in 1897, where they were assembled. They were well armed, with 12-pdr quick-firing guns in their bow and stern, as well as Maxim machine guns mounted in their after superstructure, and abaft the bridge. They were built using steel, so were proof against small-arms, and had high loopholed bulwarks, making them ideal for the task they faced.

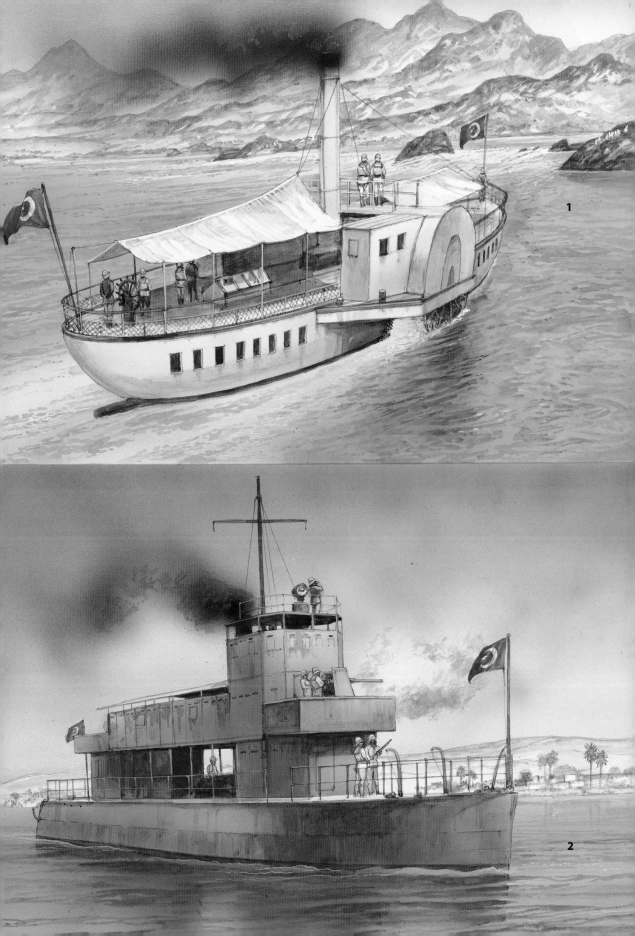

Soldiers of the 2nd Battalion Lancashire Fusiliers being crammed onto small river steamers at Wad el Abid for the final leg of their journey upriver, in late August 1898. While the bulk of the army marched up the western bank of the Nile, a small force of overcrowded transports accompanied the gunboats as they steamed upriver towards Omdurman.

overpowering, and the rats legion and ubiquitous – no place or person was too sacred for them. It is difficult to describe the state to which the Sudanese had brought the steamers during the five months they had lived as river pirates on the Nile.' This accusation of piracy is unkind – in fact the gunboats were merely operating from Shendi, beyond the command reach of Gordon in Khartoum. The rats though, were a major problem, and scurried around the ships with little regard for the vessels' human occupants.

This description is in marked contrast to the state of the gunboats serving under Kitchener's command in 1896–98. Kitchener's gunboats were run on British lines, though with a largely native crew, who were made to swab the decks every morning, and to develop a pride in the appearance of their vessels. Naval officers, petty officers and selected leading hands rather than native officers commanded the Egyptian or Sudanese boat crew; Royal Marine and army NCOs oversaw the Egyptian army gun crews and any embarked Egyptian troops; and both naval and civilian engineers supervised the native stokers. There was no room for filth, rats or poorly stowed crates of stores.

Even when army contingents with their own officers and NCOs were embarked, conditions on board were clearly different to life in the 'penny steamers'. On every gunboat that served on the Nile from the Tamai-class onwards, there were proper 'earth boxes' (toilets) near the stern, wash rooms, cabins, and a galley. Officers and NCOs had their own wardroom and senior rates' mess respectively, and native servants were on hand to attend to their needs. Above all, naval traditions were imposed, in everything from the daily

On the *Bordein*, a howitzer is deployed to starboard, while picked marksmen from the Royal Sussex Regiment fire at the enemy on either shore. This engraving depicts the moment when the little steamer approached Tuti Island near Khartoum – a stretch of the river which was heavily defended by the Mahdists, and the passage was made under a very heavy fire.

rum issue (to British servicemen only), to discipline on board, and even the rations, which were supplied by the army commissariat, but eaten by British and natives alike in naval fashion, by 'messes'. Above all, the ships were commanded by experienced naval officers, or in a few cases Royal Engineers.

Many of those who served in the 1896–98 campaigns went on to hold high command. For instance, Lieutenant David Beatty commanded the *El Fateh*, among others, Lieutenant Walter Cowan commanded the *Sultan*, Lieutenant Cecil Staveley the *Hafir*, Lieutenant the Honourable Horace Hood the *El Nasir*, and Commander Colin Keppel – the flotilla commander – flew his flag in the *El Zafir*. All would hold flag rank during World War I. Beatty commanded the British Battlecruiser Fleet at the battle of Jutland in 1916, and Hood lost his life when his flagship *Invincible* blew up during the same battle.

Firepower

There was a considerable difference between the weaponry employed in the steamers used in the 1884–85 campaign and those which saw action during the campaign of 1896–98. This is hardly surprising as General Gordon had very limited resources in Khartoum to draw upon, while in the later campaign, Kitchener had the wealth of an Empire at his disposal, and so his gunboats – 'Kitchener's toys' as the press initially dubbed them – lacked little in the way of ordnance.

Colonel Sir Charles Wilson said of the weaponry available to him during 'The River Dash':

This sketch by a British officer shows the scene amidships on the *Bordein* during January–February 1885. Men of the Naval Brigade man a Nordenfelt gun on a firing platform above the waist, while below them their shipmates engage the enemy with rifle fire. The wooden-walled structure above the after superstructure and wheel can be seen further aft.

Our guns were what the French call *canons rayés*, small handy brass pieces, throwing a 9-pound shell, and the soldiers were armed with Remingtons, but instead of a bayonet each man had a spear, and many of them swords as well. Many of the men wore Gordon's decoration for the siege of Khartoum, of which they were very proud. There was an abundance of gun and small-arms ammunition, and Gordon had evidently spared no trouble in making the steamers as good fighting boats as possible. If there had only been officers and men of the Naval Brigade to man them, it would have been perfect.

These 9-pdr guns were small bronze muzzle-loading rifled shell howitzers, produced in 1859, and bought from the French by the Egyptian government during the late 1860s. It was a weapon of the La Hitte system, *a canon de campagne*, with an 86mm (3.4in) bore, and had a barrel length of just 1.43m (4ft 8in). The gun fired a rifled shell, and was accurate at ranges in excess of 1,000 yards. While Wilson's ships *Bordein* and *Talahawiyeh* lacked machine guns, the *Safia* was armed with Gardners, and accounts from near Khartoum in late 1884

The Melik and her sister ships of the Sultan-class were built specifically for service on the river Nile, and to participate in the reconquest of the Sudan. They were therefore designed to be shallow-drafted, but they were also powered by significantly more effective engines than previous gunboats, in order to better hold their position in the river while pointing upstream,

and to push their way more effectively through its many cataracts. The vessels were well-protected – effectively proof against enemy rifle fire – while their powerful armament of quick-firing guns and modern machine guns was meant to overwhelm enemy positions on the river bank. In other words, the *Melik* was the ultimate Nile river gunboat.

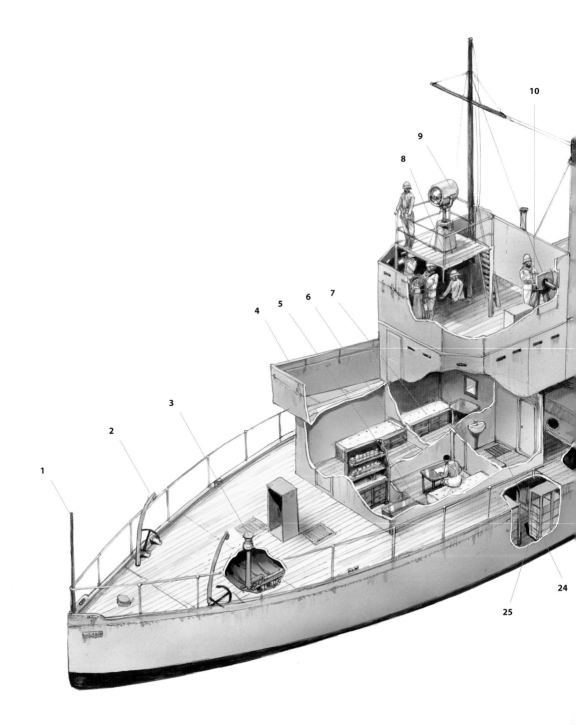

KEY

1. Jack staff
2. Anchor davits
3. Capstan
4. Forward 12-pdr QF gun (not visible)
5. Wardroom
6. Officers' accommodation
7. Commander's cabin
8. Bridge and wheelhouse
9. Searchlight

10. Bridge-mounted Maxim machine gun (one of two)
11. Battery deck Maxim machine gun (one of four)
12. After steering position
13. After 12-pdr QF gun
14. Ensign staff
15. Rudder
16. Heads (below upper deck)
17. Propeller (one of two)

18. Crew's messdeck (below upper deck)
19. Pantry and washrooms
20. Engineers' mess
21. After magazine
22. Triple-expansion engine (one of two)
23. Boiler (one of two)
24. Officers' washroom
25. Forward magazine

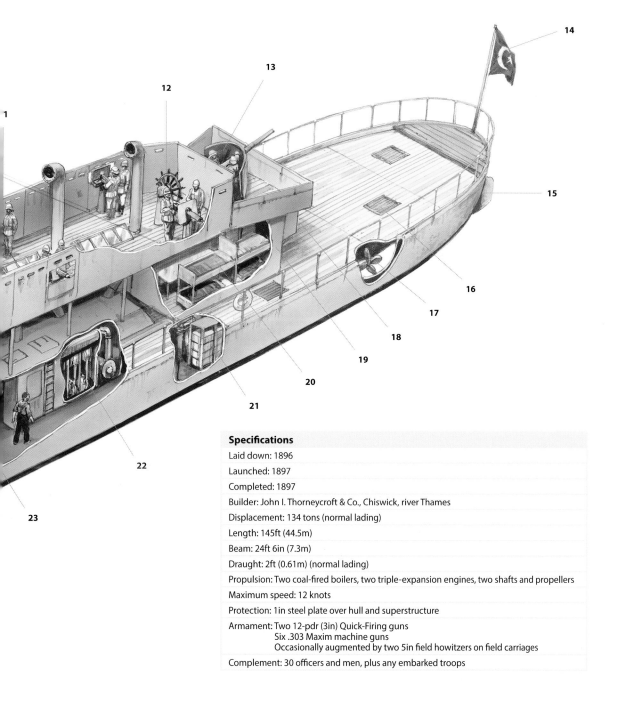

Specifications	
Laid down: 1896	
Launched: 1897	
Completed: 1897	
Builder: John I. Thorneycroft & Co., Chiswick, river Thames	
Displacement: 134 tons (normal lading)	
Length: 145ft (44.5m)	
Beam: 24ft 6in (7.3m)	
Draught: 2ft (0.61m) (normal lading)	
Propulsion: Two coal-fired boilers, two triple-expansion engines, two shafts and propellers	
Maximum speed: 12 knots	
Protection: 1in steel plate over hull and superstructure	
Armament: Two 12-pdr (3in) Quick-Firing guns Six .303 Maxim machine guns Occasionally augmented by two 5in field howitzers on field carriages	
Complement: 30 officers and men, plus any embarked troops	

suggest that the 'penny steamer' flotilla might have employed either Gardner or Nordenfelt machine guns or both, in very limited numbers. Unlike the *Safia*'s Gardners, which were supplied by the Royal Navy, these weapons would have been owned and operated by the Egyptian army.

The Gardner was developed in 1874 by William Gardner of Toledo, Ohio. Unlike later variants these Gardner machine guns were single-barrelled weapons, operated by means of a hand crank, and with the mechanism fed from an overhead magazine. The Swedish-designed but British-built Nordenfelt was a similar weapon that entered service at the same time, but it had multiple barrels – usually five of them. It was fed from an overhead hopper, and was operated by a hand-pulled lever. In theory, both of these weapons had a high rate of fire, but the speed depended on the ability of the gunner to operate the handle. While their manufacturers of both weapons claimed they could fire thousands of rounds without jamming, in fact conditions in the Sudan (where sand clogged the mechanisms) meant that both weapons were prone to malfunction.

These hand-operated machine guns were superseded during the 1880s by a new machine gun designed by Sir Hiram Maxim, an American who lived in Great Britain. Trials showed that his weapon could fire 600 rounds per minute, and as the weapon was powered by the gas recoil of the previous round, all the gunner had to do was pull the trigger. This modern machine gun effectively rendered all earlier hand-operated weapons obsolete. It was used to great effect during the campaigns of 1896–98, mounted on Kitchener's river gunboats in batteries of two or more weapons on each side of a gun deck.

In all these cases the machine guns were primarily used to suppress enemy gun batteries, thereby allowing gunners to destroy the enemy gun itself through counter-battery fire. However, at Shendi, Maxims were used to clear enemy riflemen hiding in trees, while at Omdurman they were used to engage fleeing Mahdists.

An equally useful weapon designed by Maxim was the 1-pdr 'pom-pom'. Introduced during the 1890s, this 37mm (1.46in)-calibre Maxim-Nordenfelt was the first automatic cannon – a larger version of the machine gun, but capable of firing exploding shells. It had an effective range of approximately 2,500 yards and a theoretical rate of fire of up to 300 rounds per minute. In reality it was fired at a much slower rate, hence the 'pom pom' of its nickname – the sound it made as it fired. It proved ideal for smothering Mahdist gun positions with fast, accurate fire.

The largest weapon carried in these later gunboats was the 12-pdr 12 cwt (hundredweight) QF (quick-firing) gun Mark I. It was a 3in (76mm)-calibre weapon, 10ft 4in long, and weighing 0.6 tons (610kg) It was a rifled breech-loading gun, and therefore had a high rate of fire – up to 15 rounds a minute in well-trained hands – and impressive accuracy. First introduced into naval service in 1895, all the gunboats of the flotilla were armed with this weapon – those vessels already in service as well as those still being built. It had a maximum range of 11,750 yards (10,740m), and could fire both high-explosive and shrapnel rounds. In naval service armour-piercing rounds were also issued, but of course these were of little use on the Nile.

Finally, some of the Nile gunboats were armed with field artillery to augment their firepower. On Gordon's gunboats this was the 90mm C73 Krupp field gun, a weapon first introduced in 1873, and sold to the Egyptian

Manhandling a Nordenfelt onto a river transport at Gubat, in preparation for 'The River Dash', January 1885. These transports and the gunboats escorting them were to forge ahead upriver, in an attempt to relieve Khartoum before the Desert Column reached the city.

government. It was a breech-loading weapon with a sliding block, cast in steel, which fired an 88mm shell, with a maximum range of 7,100 yards (6,500m). Both high-explosive and shrapnel rounds were available. The shell was loaded, followed by a powder bag, and a friction tube was used to fire the piece. These were occasionally emplaced in the bow 'turrets' of Gordon's steamers, still on their standard two-wheeled Egyptian army carriage. These weapons were crewed by Egyptian gunners, who were considered reasonably proficient at their trade. For a few years they were also mounted in the Tamai-class gunboats, on naval-style mountings manufactured especially in Cairo.

In the later gunboats, a British BL 5in (127mm) howitzer was sometimes embarked, together with its British or Egyptian gun crew. Like the Krupp weapon this was a breech-loader, with an interrupted screw mechanism, and used a separate shell and powder charge. It fired a 50lb shell, and both Common (high-explosive) shells and the new and more powerful Lyddite shells were available. It had a range of 4,800 yards (4,400m), and was mounted on a standard two-wheeled field carriage. Its only real disadvantage was its weight. At 2,672lb (1.2 tons, or 1,212kg), it significantly added to the weight of the gunboat, and so care had to be taken in its emplacement on board. However, it provided considerable additional firepower to the vessel; it effectively doubled the number of heavy guns on board a Sultan-class gunboat, and was larger and more powerful than the 12-pdrs, although with one-third of their rate of fire. Usually, one was mounted on the quarterdeck, and another on the forecastle.

GUNBOATS IN ACTION

The 1884–85 campaign

When General Gordon reached the Sudan in February 1884, he made good use of his small flotilla of makeshift Egyptian gunboats, employing them to patrol the Upper Nile and augment the defences of Khartoum. That December, when the city was besieged, he sent four of them downriver to rendezvous

An armed government steamer off Gubat near Mettemeh, about 80 miles below Khartoum, and below the Sixth Cataract. It was here that part of the Gordon relief force embarked, and 'The River Dash' began. Behind the gunboat two barges can be seen, while the relief force's defended encampment can be seen on the bluffs overlooking the landing place.

with the approaching relief expedition. They met Colonel Sir Charles Wilson's Desert Column near Metemmeh, but Wilson was short of men and supplies, and was still waiting for the River Column to catch him up. Nevertheless, he decided to take the gunboats *Bordein* and *Talahawiyeh* upriver, in an attempt to rescue Gordon. What became known as 'The River Dash' began on 24 January 1885, and the following day the steamers passed through the hazardous Sixth Cataract without serious incident, despite the *Bordein* grazing the rocks. On the morning of 28 January Khartoum was sighted, but the Egyptian flag was no longer flying over the Governor's House – a clear sign that Khartoum had fallen, and that Gordon was dead. They were too late. Here, Wilson described the situation:

> Directly after, a heavy fire was opened upon us from four guns and many rifles at from 600 to 700 yards. The guns were well-placed … the bullets began to fly thickly, tapping like hail against the ship's sides, while the shells went screeching overhead, or threw up jets of water round us. Our men replied cheerily, and the gun in the turret was capitally served by the black gunners

E

ABU KLEA AND *HAFIR*, KHARTOUM, 1900

The *Abu Klea* and the *Hafir* were both Tamai-class river gunboats. Together with their sister ships, the *Tamai* and the *Metemmeh*, they were dubbed 'small sternwheelers', to differentiate them from the *El Zafir* and her two sisters, which were referred to as 'large sternwheelers'. All four Tamai-class vessels entered service in 1885, but saw no action until 1896, when they took part in the Dongola campaign. The *Hafir* was originally called the *El Teb*, but she was renamed in 1897, on the eve of the final conquest of the Sudan. From 1894 on, the vessels were armed with a 12-pdr gun, a 1-pdr 'pom-pom' and four Maxim machine guns.

This scene shows the two gunboats tied up alongside Khartoum's 'Gunboat Station', which was located on the Blue Nile, in front of the Governor's House. Here the vessels are moored to posts sunk in the river, but they could just as easily be tied to the shore, or to floating pontoons. An army sentry guards the 'brow' or gangway linking the gunboats to the shore, to keep the locals at bay. This bow-to-stern form of mooring alongside each other, which can be seen in contemporary photographs, was probably done to prevent accidental damage to the paddlewheel boxes if the vessels banged against each other in the current. The lack of clutter on board and the smart rig of the sailors suggests that the vessels are about to be inspected. On patrol these vessels would be littered with stores, embarked troops and even extra guns.

The rendezvous between the River Column and the Desert Column at Gubat near Metemmeh, 21 January 1885, with the gunboats *Bordein*, *Talahawiyeh*, *Sāfia* and *Tawfiqiyeh* in the lead. The Desert Column had just defeated the Mahdists at the battle of Abu Klea, and were preparing to clear Metemmeh when the River Column arrived.

under their captain … the gunners, who had nothing on but a cloth around their waists, looked more like demons than men in the thick smoke … The shooting was fairly good, and we heard afterwards that we had dismounted one of the guns in the battery.

After this dramatic battle with the Mahdist batteries Wilson headed back down the Nile. They had been lucky to escape serious damage, but the following day their luck ran out. On 29 January the *Talahawiyeh* struck a rock and sank, but not before her crew were rescued by the *Bordein*. Two days later, on 31 January, the overcrowded *Bordein* struck another rock off Mernat Island, and had to be beached. His now disaffected native troops refused to move off the island, so Wilson built a defensive *zariba*, and sent an officer downriver in a rowing boat, to find help. At dawn on 1 February it came upon Captain Lord Charles Beresford RN in the *Safīa*, who had embarked 20 soldiers and headed upstream. On 3 February they were engaged by a Mahdist battery, and soon found themselves in serious difficulty. Here, Beresford recounts the battle that followed:

The *Safieh* was simply a penny steamer in a packing-case. Where the packing-case was deficient, bullets went through her as through paper, and a shell would pierce her wooden jacket. On 1st February we shoved along at the rate of 2.5 miles an hour, the most the *Safieh* could do against the current, stopped to get wood, and anchored in the stream during the night. It was impossible to navigate in the dark … At 7 am [3 February] we sighted Wad Habeshi on the starboard hand… Wad Habeshi was a strong earthwork, with four embrasures, mounting four guns … the only practicable channel ran within eighty yards of the fort. We could only crawl past the battery, and as we were defenceless against gun-fire, our only chance was to maintain so overwhelming a fire upon the embrasures as to demoralise the guns' crews. It was an extreme instance of the principle that the best defence resides in gun-fire rather than in armour; for we had no effective armour.

Accordingly, the starboard Gardner and the two brass guns, the 20 soldiers and 14 bluejackets, poured a steady and an accurate fire into the fort, disregarding the parties of riflemen who were shooting at us from the bank….

so deadly was the fire we poured into the embrasures of the fort, that the enemy could not fire the two guns bearing upon the *Safieh* while she was bore abeam of them. We passed the fort, and by the time we had left it about 200 yards astern, our fire necessarily slackened, as our guns no longer bore upon the battery. Suddenly a great cloud of steam or smoke rose from the after hatchway. Instantly the fire of the enemy increased. Chief Engineer Benbow, who was standing with me on the quarter-deck, ran to the engine-room … I saw the black stokers rushing up from the stoke-hold hatchway. At the moment it was uncertain whether the ship was on fire or the boiler injured; but as she still had way upon her I ordered her to be headed towards the bank, away from the fort, and so gained another few yards…

In the meantime our fire upon the side embrasure of the fort was continued by the riflemen; and it went on without pause, lest the enemy should get another shot in. I dropped anchor, and addressed the men. I told them that the vessel was all right, as she had only a foot of water under her bottom... I asked Mr. Benbow if he could repair the boiler. He replied, 'I think I can do it' … at any moment another shell might burst into the engine-room. But Mr. Benbow went on with his work. On deck, we continued to maintain a steady fire, hour after hour, upon the fort. It was our only chance. The slightest cessation, and they would bring their gun to bear on us.... The fire from the Gardner and the rifle-fire, directed upon the side embrasure of the fort, were so accurate and incessant that the gunners of the enemy never had a chance, either to get their gun to bear or to remove it to another position. The few shots they fired travelled about 100 yards to the right of the steamer. Meantime, Mr. Benbow, down below, went on with his work.

The small flotilla of Khartoum-based Egyptian government river steamers were hastily armed and played a vital role in the defence of the city, by engaging Mahdist strongpoints along the banks of the Nile, and preventing enemy use of the river.

After Chief Engineer Benbow managed to patch the boiler the gunboat limped away upriver, and linked up with Wilson's stranded party. The now dangerously overloaded *Safia* ran downstream again, passing the battery, and on 4 February Beresford and Wilson reached the safety of Metemmeh. Wilson soon found that General Wolseley had made him the scapegoat for the expedition's failure, and while he never held an active command again, public disapprobation ensured that Wolseley's days of campaigning were over too. Six months later the Mahdi died, and the Khalifa Abdulla el-Taishi assumed command of the Mahdists. He attempted an invasion of Egypt in 1889, but the three Tamai-class gunboats based near Wadi Halfa helped ensure this came to nothing. The Khalifa then devoted his energy to massacring his political and religious opponents, and launching desultory attacks on Christian Abyssinia. It has been estimated that during his 13 years in power a combination of disease and massacres reduced the population of the Sudan by almost two-thirds.

On 29 January 1885, during 'The River Dash', the small gunboat *Sāfia*, commanded by Lord Charles Beresford RN, ran aground in front of the Mahdist guns on Wad Habeshi. Her two brass 4-pdrs returned the enemy fire, supported by Gardner machine guns, and the duel continued until nightfall. She was finally extricated the following day.

The 1896–98 campaign

At first the British government seemed happy to leave the Sudan well alone, but by 1896 political pressure, spurred by the threat of French intervention in the region, led to the decision to reclaim the Sudan. So, in March 1896, the Sirdar (commander-in-chief) of the Egyptian Army, General Kitchener, crossed the border into the Northern Sudan, supported by a flotilla of four Tamai-class gunboats. What followed became known as the Dongola campaign, after the Sudanese province where the fighting took place. After an initial skirmish at Firket in early June the advance was halted due to an outbreak of cholera. However, on 18 September *Tamai*, *Abu Klea* and *Metemmeh* went into action near the village of Hafir. After shooting up a group of Mahdist supply boats they came under heavy fire from the village. Winston Churchill described the fight in *The River War*:

> As the gunboats approached the northern end they opened fire with their guns, striking the mud entrenchments at every shot, and driving clouds of dust and splinters into the air. The Maxim guns began to search the parapets, and two companies of the Staffordshire Regiment on board the unarmoured steamers *Dal* and *Akasha* fired long-range volleys… As they came opposite Hafir, where the channel narrows to about 600 yards, they were received by a very heavy fire from guns placed in cleverly screened batteries, and from the riflemen

GUNBOAT IN ACTION OFF KHARTOUM, 1884

This scene, based on contemporary accounts, and on dramatic engravings, shows the Egyptian gunboats engaging the Mahdists besieging Khartoum. It shows the bows of a gunboat such as the *Safia* or, more likely, the *Mansoura*, which were fitted with improvised bulwarks made from baulks of timber. On 10 September both of them escorted the *Abbās* as she broke through the siege lines and headed downriver for help. They continued as far as Berber, when the two escorts returned to Khartoum. This shows one of them engaging Mahdist batteries near Egeiga, 15 miles downriver from Khartoum.

In this scene a British army officer tries to spot the position of Mahdist guns near the village, while Egyptian troops armed with Remington breech-loading rifles engage the Mahdists firing at them from both banks of the Nile. In the bow a 90mm Krupp breech-loading field gun has been mounted, protected by a steel mantlet and sandbags. Although it is incapable of being traversed to the beam, it still has a reasonable angle of fire. As there is insufficient steel plate to line the bulwarks, gaps in the makeshift parapet are filled by sandbags.

A small armed sternwheel steamer of the Egyptian government, which took part in the 1898 campaign. She is most probably the *Metemmeh*, which was initially armed with a single 90mm Krupp gun in the bow, as well as machine guns on either beam.

Officers of the 5th Northumberland Regiment, pictured on board one of the three Sultan-class gunboats during the 1898 campaign. They formed part of the army detachment embarked in both transports and gunboats for the final advance on Omdurman in late August.

sheltered in deep pits by the water's edge or concealed amid the foliage of the tops of the palm-trees. These aerial skirmishers commanded the decks of the vessels, and the shields of the guns were thus rendered of little protection. All the water round the gunboats was torn into foam by the projectiles. The bullets pattered against their sides, and, except where they were protected by steel plates, penetrated. One shell struck the *Abu Klea* on the water-line, and entered the magazine. Luckily it did not explode, the Dervishes having forgotten to set the fuse.

Three shells struck the *Metemma*. On board the *Tamai*, which was leading, Commander Colville was severely wounded in the wrist; Armourer-Sergeant Richardson was killed at his Maxim gun, and on each boat some casualties occurred. So hot was the fire that it was thought doubtful whether to proceed with the bombardment, and the *Tamai* swung round, and hurried down the river with the current and at full steam to report to the Sirdar. The other gunboats remained in action, and continued to shell the Dervish defences. The *Tamai* soon returned to the fight, and, steaming again up the river, was immediately hotly re-engaged. The sight which the army witnessed was thrilling… By the Nile all the tops of the palm-trees were crowded with daring riflemen, whose positions were indicated by the smoke-puffs of their rifles, or when some tiny black figure fell, like a shot rook, to the ground. In the foreground the gunboats, panting and puffing up the river, were surrounded on all sides by spouts and spurts of water, thrown up by the shells and bullets. Again the flotilla drew near the narrow channel; again the watching army held their breath; and again they saw the leading boat, the *Metemma*, turn and run down stream towards safety, pursued by the wild cheers of the Arabs. It was evident that the gunboats were not strong enough to silence the Dervish fire.

Despite the *Metemmeh* being forced to withdraw downriver, the *Tamai* and *Abu Klea* eventually fought their way past the batteries and anchored upstream of them. The village was abandoned in the night, and the gunboat flotilla continued on to Dongola, which they bombarded, forcing the Mahdists to evacuate the town. This effectively completed this opening campaign of the war. During the lull that followed, Kitchener began building his supply railway from Wadi Halfa on the Egyptian border towards Abu Hamed on the Upper Nile, above the Fourth Cataract. The gunboat flotilla was also reinforced, with the arrival of three 'large sternwheelers' – *El Zafir*, *El Nasir* and *El Fateh*.

In August 1897 the invasion was resumed, and Abu Hamed was captured after a brisk fight. Berber fell soon afterwards, and the gunboats were ordered forward past the Fourth Cataract. Lieutenant Beatty's *Hafir* (formerly the *El Teb*) was wrecked there, but by the end of August five gunboats reached their new forward base at Abu Hamed. The next part of the advance could now begin.

In mid-October the three new El Zafir-class gunboats under the command of Commander Keppel went into action for the first time off Shendi, the fortified position that controlled the approach to Metemmeh. It was defended by a large Mahdist force commanded by the Emir Mahmud – the cousin of the Khalifa – and the gunboats bombarded the fort, while Egyptian troops attacked the position from the north. Again, Churchill described the fight:

On the 14th [October] the *Zafir*, *Fateh*, and *Naser* steamed south from Berber, under Commander Keppel, each carrying, besides its ordinary native crew, fifty men of the IXth Soudanese and two British sergeants of Marine Artillery. Shortly after daybreak on the 16th the flotilla approached the enemy's position. So silently had they moved that a small Dervish outpost a few miles to the north of Shendi was surprised still sleeping, and the negligent guards, aroused by a splutter of firing from the Maxim guns, awoke to find three terrible machines close upon them. The gunboats pursued their way, and, disdaining a few shots which were fired from the ruins of Shendi, arrived, at about seven o'clock, within range of Metemma. The town itself stood more than a thousand yards from the Nile, but six substantial mud forts, armed with artillery, lined and defended the riverside.

Creeping leisurely forward along the east bank, remote from the Dervish works, the flotilla came into action at a range of 4,000 yards. The fire was at first concentrated on the two northern forts, and the shells, striking the mud walls in rapid succession or bursting in the interior, soon enveloped them in dust and smoke. The Dervishes immediately replied, but the inferiority of their skill and weapons was marked, and, although their projectiles reached the flotilla, very few took effect. One shell, however, crashed through the deck of the *Zafir*, mortally wounding a Soudanese soldier, and two struck the *Fateh*. After the long-range bombardment had continued for about an hour the gunboats moved forward opposite to the enemy's position, and poured a heavy and continuous fire of shrapnel and double shell into all the forts, gradually subduing their resistance. The fugitives from the batteries, and small parties of Baggara horse who galloped about on the open plain between the works and the town, afforded good targets to the Maxims, and many were licked up even at extreme ranges. No sooner had the gunboats passed the forts than the Dervish fire ceased entirely, and it was discovered that their embrasures only commanded the northern approach. As the guns could not be pointed to the southward, the flotilla need fear nothing from any fort that had been left behind.

Shendi fell after two days of almost continual fighting. The army paused there to await the completion of the railway, which after reaching Abu Hamed was

During the advance on Dongola in mid-September 1896, after negotiating the Third Cataract the leading gunboats of the river fleet were lashed to river dhows, to give some additional protection to their hulls. In fact, when the flotilla engaged the enemy on 18 September, the fire was so heavy they were forced to withdraw. Here the flagship *Tamai* leads the way, followed by the *Abu Klea*. The engraver captioned her as the *El Teb*, but she was still negotiating the Third Cataract when the action took place.

The river transports and escorting river transports of Major-General Kitchener's Anglo-Egyptian army leaving Mernat Island and beginning their final advance towards Omdurman in late August 1898. A gunboat – the *Melik* – is in the lead, while astern of her the *Sultan* and the *Sheikh* escort three sternwheel transports. A smaller unidentified gunboat brings up the rear.

extended as far as Ababiya, then Berber and Atbara. During this pause the army was reinforced by a brigade of British regulars, and on 8 April they engaged and defeated the Mahdists at the battle of Atbara. The river Atbara was too shallow for the gunboats to support this operation, but they patrolled aggressively up the Nile, as far as the Sixth Cataract. It was soon found that the Mahdists had fallen back, and were reforming their army at Omdurman. Another lull followed, during which another British brigade arrived, and the gunboat flotilla was reinforced by three new vessels of the Sultan-class – *Sultan*, *Sheikh* and *Melik*. They would prove invaluable in what came next.

In late August at Wad Hamed Kitchener divided his army into a land column and a small river one – the latter consisting of river transports carrying 250 men, protected by the gunboats. They advanced to the Sixth Cataract, where the confined Shabukla Gorge proved to be undefended. However, as the flotilla negotiated the Sixth Cataract Keppel's flagship *El Zafir* struck a rock, and sank. Her crew were lucky to escape with their lives. The *Hafir* was still being raised, so that left Keppel with eight of his ten gunboats available for the final phase of the campaign.

By 1 September the main army was less than seven miles from Omdurman, while the gunboats steamed on to engage Mahdist positions on the eastern bank of the Nile. When the eastern bank was cleared a battery of Royal Artillery howitzers was landed there, and together with the three Sultan-class gunboats they bombarded Mahdist batteries at Omdurman itself. Some were clustered beside the Mahdi's tomb, which was heavily damaged in the fighting. However, the Mahdist guns had been silenced.

That night the gunboats used their searchlights to play over the Mahdist encampment, and to sweep the ground in front of Kitchener's army, which

G *MELIK* IN ACTION OFF OMDURMAN, 1898

The last stage of Major-General Kitchener's advance on Omdurman was spearheaded by the gunboat flotilla. At its head were the three powerful Sultan-class vessels *Sultan*, *Melik* and *Sheikh*. On 1 September 1898 these gunboats approached Omdurman, where they were engaged by Mahdist riflemen and gun batteries. The enemy rifle fire proved ineffective, while the enemy batteries were eventually silenced by the gunboat's suite of two quick-firing 12-pdr (3in) guns. They forged on to within sight of the Mahdi's tomb, across the river from Khartoum. There they were joined by other gunboats, including the *El Zafir*. After silencing all enemy opposition, they returned downriver to Egeiga, where Kitchener's army disembarked. The following day the gunboats were in action again, firing into the flank of the Mahdist army as it threw itself on the British defences around Egeiga, in what became known as the battle of Omdurman.

This scene shows the *Melik* making her way upriver towards Omdurman on the morning of 1 September. She is firing both of her 12-pdrs at the enemy, while Maxim guns mounted on her battery deck and beneath her bridge add to the carnage. In addition, British soldiers also fire at the enemy, from loopholes cut in the protective steel sides of the vessel's superstructure. With their 180-degree arc of fire, the 12-pdrs were capable of firing to either side, as well as forward or aft of the vessel. This made the *Melik* and her well-armed sisters the perfect vessels to spearhead the drive on Omdurman.

The Sultan-class gunboat *Melik*, as she appeared at the end of the 1898 campaign. Her usually spacious quarterdeck is cluttered with embarked stores and ordnance, which suggests the photograph was taken soon after the recapture of Khartoum, when she was used to transport troops to harry the dispersed remnants of the Mahdist army.

was now in a defensive *zariba* near Egeiga, to the north of the city. This probably discouraged a Mahdist night attack. When the attack came the following morning, 2 September, the Mahdists were slaughtered.

The battle of Omdurman, fought on the plains of Kerreri, was a one-sided affair. Anglo-Egyptian losses were negligible, while the Khalifa lost a quarter of his 55,000-strong army killed, with as many more wounded. The gunboats played their part in the battle, using their guns to support the Camel Corps and the Egyptian cavalry, and the foolhardy charge of the 21st Lancers, and then to harry the enemy as they were routed from the battlefield.

Effectively the campaign ended that day, although it would be another year before the Khalifa was cornered and killed, and the last of his army destroyed. During this time the gunboats patrolled the Blue and White Niles, and helping to pacify the rest of the country.

The gunboat *Bordein* as she looks today, in Khartoum. She had lain abandoned there since World War II, but in 2006 she was saved from the scrapyard. Unfortunately despite plans for her restoration, she still remains in this dilapidated condition. (The Melik Society)

FURTHER READING

Beresford, Lord Charles, *The Memoirs of Admiral Lord Beresford* (Boston, MA, 1914, Little Brown & Co.)

Butler, Sir William F., *The Campaign of the Cataracts* (London, 2010, Kessinger Publishing. First published London, 1887)

Churchill, Winston S., *The River War: An Account of the Reconquest of the Soudan* (New York, NY, 2013, Skyhorse Publishing. First published London, 1899)

Colville, H.E., *History of the Sudan Campaigns* (London, 1889, War Office)

Gardiner, Robert (ed.), *Conway's All the World's Fighting Ships, 1906–1921* (London, 1985, Conway Maritime Press)

Gardiner, Robert (ed.), *The Advent of Steam: The Merchant Steamship before 1900* (London, 1992, Conway Maritime Press)

Keown-Boyd, Henry, *A Good Dusting: The Sudan Campaigns, 1883–1899* (London, 1986, Leo Cooper)

Snook, Mike, *Go Strong in the Desert: the Mahdist uprising in the Sudan, 1881–85* (Nottingham, 2010, Perry Miniatures)

Wilson, Sir Charles W., *From Korti to Khartum* (Uxfield, East Sussex, 2009, Naval & Military Press (First published Edinburgh, 1885)

Wood, Sir Evelyn, *Midshipman to Field Marshal* (Charleston, SC, 2012, Nabu Press. First published London, 1906)

Journals

As little has been published on these vessels, the following journals are particularly relevant:

Gunboat: Journal of the Melik Society

Sudan Notes and Records Navy and Army Illustrated

The Melik Society

This worthy organisation aims to advance awareness of Anglo-Sudanese history through the restoration and preservation of the Nile river gunboats *Melik* and *Bordein*.

For more information, visit www.melik.org.uk

The last surviving working gunboat on the Nile was the *Melik*. She remained in service until 1926, and was briefly restored to duty during World War II. She subsequently became the clubhouse of the Blue Nile Sailing Club, but today she lies abandoned, despite plans by the Melik Society to preserve and restore her. (The Melik Society)

INDEX